Locked In

Build a Business
Build a Brand

Presented by Konnect Four

Table of Contents

Getting Started

Most people have no idea on how to start a business. You have tons of ideas in your head and everything seems like it would work out in the long run however, the big question is, where do you begin? The initial stages of a startup can be overwhelming. There is a lot of planning and outlining that needs to take place as well as having all the resources to plant the seed. As stated in our previous book, proper prior planning prevents piss poor performance. Having a silicon plan is the basis of any start up business. Why silicon? Well, silicon is flexible yet durable. You want to have a firm plan, but at the same time, you want to allow some flexibility just in case things do not go as originally planned. Let's look at a few things to consider upon starting your own business.

- Type of Business
- Resources Available
- Initial Business Plan or Proposal
- Expenses
- Your Availability and Time

Type of Business

Do you want to offer a product or service as apart of your business? A service is considered something that a person needs or seeks out but is not necessarily a tangible item. Hair salon, computer repair, pest control, and housekeeping are some examples of a service. A product on the other hand, is a tangible item that can be bought and taken with the consumer. Blow dryer, laptop, bug spray, and vacuum are examples of a product.

Resources Available

Gathering all your available resources ahead of time will be beneficial to your start up business. Your business may require a certain dollar amount in order to get started; you need to make sure you are ready to make that investment. Consider getting a mentor or someone to help consult you along the way. Joining a local business club or group via social media, could save you time in the steps you need to get started on your own. There are tons of resources at your fingertips that you may not realize initially, so take the time to sit down and collect them respectively.

Initial Business Plan or Proposal

You may not have $50,000 cash available to launch a new business from the ground up. Most people do not make that much money in a year of working full time! By having a business plan, you can propose your idea(s) to potential investors. The business plan should outline your line of business, the target market, any research you have done in that market, the price points, and how your company will produce profits or a return on investment for your investors. It's best to draft a business plan and review it with a close resource or a private consulting company.

Expenses

Spending money on a new business is easy to do and the costs can add up quickly. Consider any expenses you can foresee in starting your business. A few basic expenses may include:
- Website
- Logo
- Business cards
- Product related costs
- Service related costs
- Office Space / Rent fees
- Advertisement

Keep in mind, nothing in life is free and neither is starting a business. You must be prepared to spend some type of money in the beginning and plan to keep that money vested into your business until profits start to roll in. Planning for expenses will save you a headache later on.

Your Availability and Time

The time you have set aside to start your business is critical. Work, school, and personal life can have an effect on the development of your business. Make sure you allow proper time to work on things pertaining to starting your business. Do not try to do everything in one day. Be proactive and plan out your day/week and incorporate "business time" into that plan. Good time management skills will be an asset to your business as well as your personal life.

These five items are critical to the birth of your new business. A simple idea is nothing without any action behind it. Taking the time to gather these few items and document them, will save you time and stress later on. Now that we have some seeds, lets begin to plant!

Finding Your Niche

The key to a successful business and what sets some of the world's biggest companies apart from others is their niche. So what exactly is a niche? A niche in business is a focus on a specific type of product or service within a specific market segment. A niche needs to contain the following:

1. A unique product or service
2. A marketable product or service
3. A niche market that is available
4. A product or service that can be expanded later on

A unique product or service

If you want to be successful in your business, you have to be the only person selling what you are selling. For example, if you are interested in clothing design, what will set your clothing company apart from all the others. There has to be something unique about your clothes that will appeal to potential customers over another brand. One might consider clothing made from all recyclable material, travel clothing for newborns, or even comfortable yet durable clothing for construction workers. All of these are examples of a niche.

A marketable product or service

New products are created everyday by the minute. There are tons of products on the market that are also failing just as fast as they are created. The last thing you want is to fall into any category associated with failure. With about 30,000 new products being launched annually, roughly 95% of them fail. Why is that? Many products that are launched lack one simple thing, which is the fact that nobody wants it! The bottom line is, consumers are the primary source of revenue for any business or service. You must create things that appeal to the vast majority of the buying population. Having a niche is a start, but the area of focus is the building block of success. For example, creating a doorbell that can be heard from your car is definitely a niche however, who would really want or find use in a car doorbell. The purpose of a doorbell is to notify you when someone has arrived at you place of residence. A doorbell inside a car would defeat the purpose, simply because if you are not home, there isn't much you can do about it. Ensuring that your product or service is marketable to the masses will set you high up in the rankings and significantly reduce failure rate.

A niche market that is available

The niche marketplace is a much smaller market than normal. Keeping that in mind, you want to make sure the area that you point your niche antennas in, is indeed available. You never want to jump on the bandwagon of a niche market, because if you are just joining the ride, you will surely get left behind. This is where research is required immensely. You have to devote time to research your niche market including: competitors, size of the market and profitability of the market, just to name a few. There is no point in launching a business in a niche market that is oversaturated or tapped out on innovation. Don't get discouraged, regroup and just find a new niche.

A product or service that can be expanded on later on

Your primary product or service will be the forefront of your business. Let's look at Amazon, a company that started off only selling books. Book sells online was their niche market. Currently, Amazon has over 70 private label brands and over 10 subsidiary companies in their current portfolio. We can start a company focused on building websites. Now consider a website building company specifically for pet hotels. Now consider adding on a service for connecting pet owners with pet hotels. Do you see how we took one market, found a niche, and expanded the business? The time you invest in research will add great value in the sustainability of your business.

Do Your Research

Research is going to be our focus for a little bit. As stated earlier, research is going to be essential for the start of your new business. Consider your business a smoked chicken sandwich; research would be the actual chicken fillet in between the bun. That speaks to the priority of doing adequate research. Now we are faced with the challenge of determining where exactly to start with all this research. Where do we begin? What are we researching? Who can help? Research can go as in depth as you let it, but for the purposes of starting your business, lets look at some key points to research upon starting up:

- Type of Business
- Target Market
- Competition
- Source of Funding
- Tools Needed
- Supplier / Manufacturer / Distributor (if needed)
- Storage Space / Office Space

Type of Business

The type of business you decide to create should reflect your personal interest. The interest level will have a direct impact on your work ethic. If you start a business selling pet accessories, but you have never owned a pet, the chances of your business succeeding will be decreased. Having pre-knowledge about the industry you are embarking upon, gives you a competitive edge against others in your industry. We spoke earlier about finding a niche market; your overall type of business will be the parent of that niche. If you do decide to tap into a business you have no interest in personally, just know much more research will be required.

Target Market

The target market is a particular group of consumers at which a product or service is aimed. Researching your target market will help put focus on advertising tactics once your business has launched. Some things to consider when developing your target market are:
- Age
- Location

- Gender
- Income Level
- Education Level
- Ethnic Background
- Personality
- Attitude
- Lifestyle
- Values
- Interests/Hobbies

Let's say you want to develop an app to help students find a tutor. You want to target the age group of majority of students, and a specific area so you can match tutors with students. Everything you build your business around, should incorporate these factors. Your target market is what your niche focus will be. These two items go hand in hand.

Competition

Obviously there is no market if there is no competition. Researching your competitors will help gauge how to set your business apart. It helps with branding your business and it helps with crafting the edge you need to set your business apart. Gather a list of at least five competitors in your target market. Once this list has been collected, research their audience, reviews, ratings, price points, locations and affiliated businesses. These items will give you an idea of how the competitors make money and how they are doing in the market.

Source of Funding

There are many resources available to gain funding for your start up business. Private investors, crowd source funding, fundraising, family members, bank loans, and business partners are just a few. Determining how much funding you will need to start your business will help in deciding on which way to go as far as gathering initial funds. If your business requires funding outside of your reach, making a business proposal and getting private investors will be ideal. If your business requires less massive funds to start up, consider starting a savings account or getting a small business loan from a bank. Remember to use all of your resources when it comes to funding.

Tools Needed

Today's business world is mainly run via the Internet and using analytics. A start up business will not withstand without having some type of online presence. A few simple tools that you should research and acquire when starting your business are:

- Website
- Social Media Pages
- Logo Designer
- Business Card Designer
- Order Tracking Software / Booking Software
- Data Analyst

These tools will help your business stay on track by assisting in branding, having a professional appearance, staying active with your supporters and knowing what is driving traffic to your business. Most of the tools above can be done at little to no cost. Researching these things will help you determine the needs that fit best with your business. Also, hiring a business consultant will make a lot of these tasks easier.

Supplier / Manufacturer / Distributor

Your start up, depending on the industry you step into, may require you to source out a supplier, manufacturer or distributor. A supplier is a company or organization that supplies items to your business. Let's say you open a seafood restaurant, your supplier may provide you with condiments, plates, napkins, eating utensils, cups, etc. A manufacturer is a company that builds or creates a product for your business. If your line of business is a cell phone accessory business, your manufacturer may design and build your accessories and place your branding on them. A distributor works directly with you and your business. A distributor may take your product and get it to your consumers on your behalf. If you have an online store and you don't want to house product at your home address, you may source out a distributor to handle shipping out your product. There are different needs for different businesses, so conducting, as much research into each of these components as possible, will help determine what specifically you may need for your business.

Storage Space / Office Space

As mentioned earlier, if your business requires you to house product or goods, you may consider storage options. There is always the option of storing goods at your residential home, but if there is high risk of theft, damage or misuse, getting a storage warehouse may be the best solution. If your budget does not permit for a distributor, getting a storage space is the next best option. Office space may be needed if your business is in the service sector. If you are starting a tax service, or maybe even a hair salon, you need a place to host potential clients. Again, it is not practical to host clients at your residential home. Renting out an office space or building is the most professional approach in your business. Clients want to feel comfortable, safe and attended to when patronizing your business.

Research may seem overwhelming, but remember, it is the foundation to your start up business. It is the guts of your sandwich. Spending the necessary time to conduct the proper research will only add to the success of your business. Starting a business is not an easy task, and most businesses fail because of the lack of research done prior to launching. Research is a key factor; so do not forget to do it!

Do It Yourself vs. Paying Someone Else

So far, we have covered a lot of the items needed in getting your business off the ground. There is a large amount of time that is required when building a business and building a brand. It can become overwhelming at times and can even seem a little impossible. The good thing is, if you have the financial ability, there is always the option of paying someone else to do the work for you.

Benefits of Doing It Yourself
- Cost Effective
- Creative Control
- Increased Time Management Skills
- Insight on Business World
- Hands on Experience for Future Endeavors
- Ability to Make Changes Instantly
- First Hand Look on Results

Benefits of Paying Someone Else

- Less Stressful
- Increased Spare Time
- Professional Touch
- Less Room For Error
- Ability to Learn Hands On

No matter which option you choose, there are benefits on both ends of the spectrum. The decision you make will be based on your own personal beliefs and preference. There are an abundance of resources for first-time business starters, including this book, which can help you along the way. If you are not a tech savvy person and believe some aspects may be outside your scope of ability, consider hiring a business consultant.

Advertising and Marketing

Advertising and Marketing are something like the "special features" to your business. Both are key components when it comes to establishing your brand, and both are needed tools along the complex journey to building your business. Once you start to promote your business, you will learn creative ways to market to your potential customers. One thing to take note of, these are not one in the same, so let's look at the differences between the two.

Advertising

Advertising is defined as the activity or profession of producing advertisements for commercial goods or services. It is the act of calling public attention to a business. There are many forms of advertising which include:

- Newspapers
- Magazines
- Direct Mail
- Billboards
- TV Commercials
- Radio Commercials
- Online Ad Placement
- Mobile Application Ad Placement
- Word of Mouth

With all of the above methods of advertising, you want to determine what fits closely with your start up business's needs. For example, if your business is targeting a specific age group, you want to choose advertising methods that are most likely to reach them. A business or service that has a focus group of teenagers and college students, may consider online and mobile application advertising, as this group tends to utilize their cell phones more than newspapers or magazines. Advertising can become expensive, so incorporating this into your business plan and budget will allow the proper planning strategy for executing. The least expensive and most authentic form of advertisement is word of mouth. The moment someone patronizes your business and tells someone else about it, that will cost you nothing, and in return, gains you a direct lead to a new customer. Google reviews and Yelp are some well-known forms of word of mouth advertisement. The moment a review is written by a patron at a restaurant or business, everyone using those online platforms can view this information thus, spreading the word of your business so the masses can see it. The type of advertising you decide to use will require some research to be done. There are advertising companies and professionals that can aid in this part of the business. If your budget does not allow for hiring such professionals, consider starting off with the least expensive forms by using any resources you have available.

Marketing

Marketing is the action or business of promoting and selling products or services, including market research and advertising. Advertising is a component of marketing and is the main driving tool of most marketing campaigns. Marketing is the activity, set of institutions, and processes for creating, communicating, delivering, and exchanging offerings that have value for customers, clients, partners, and society at large. There are hundreds of types of marketing and for purposes of this book; we can look at seven types that are most frequently used, when starting a business.

- Brand Management
- Market Research
- Public Relations
- Advertisement
- Content Marketing
- Social Media Marketing
- Search Engine Marketing

Brand Management

What do Apple, McDonalds and Gucci all have in common? They are all major brands with millions of devoted fans that just can't seem to get enough. The brand management behind these beloved names has played a key role in cultivating their followings. In today's crowded marketplace, brand management is the daunting challenge of making a brand stand out amongst the rest. Managing your brand will be tasked with developing, communicating and managing the various elements of your brand or product. This includes activities like designing brand elements, overseeing brand communications and guiding market research.

Market Research

Market Research is creating new knowledge. In marketing, research serves to answer questions about how consumers think, feel and act. Market research is conducting studies to better understand a particular group of consumers and later analyzing the information collected. The research can look like anything from creating online surveys to conducting focus groups. This research drives the target areas of your marketing campaign.

Public Relations

Does bad press really exist? Considering that PR professionals have been debating this question since what seems like the beginning of time, the world may never know. What is clear is that public relations is all about getting people to talk about your brand—and doing what you can to ensure that talk is positive. Public Relations acts as the spokesperson for a product, person or brand. PR is responsible for getting the word out and maintaining a positive reputation in the news for your company. Some examples of Public Relations is written press releases, stories, and communicating with news professionals in order to promote a brand, service or organization.

Advertising

As we discussed earlier, advertising comes in all shapes and sizes. Advertising is the process of persuasively communicating with consumers through paid mediums. We discussed some forms of advertising and noted that it is indeed apart of the marketing branch. Be sure to put forth some effort into your advertising campaign. This is how potential customers will be informed about your business.

Content Marketing

From the podcast you listen to in the car to your favorite morning newsletter, content marketing is everywhere you look. At the heart of it all is content, which is basically anything that delivers information to an audience. The goal of content marketing is to create valuable and useful content that serves to promote a company over time. Content marketing is the task of planning, creating and distributing content. Effective content is created with the consumer in mind, so it's important the content empathizes with the audience. By engaging consumers to address their interests on an individual level, successful content will build trust between the customers and your brand.

Social Media Marketing

Social media platforms have fundamentally changed the way marketing interacts with an audience. How, you may ask? With social media, brands can reach consumers across the world at all times of day, instantly. That's a pretty big deal — even bigger is the ability for consumers to engage and instantly give feedback to marketing efforts. Social media marketing aims to leverage this massive opportunity to develop relationships with consumers, promote brand awareness and drive traffic to a website or store. Social media marketing is the complex job of managing your brand's social media presence across online platforms. This encompasses everything from responding to customer comments, to developing hashtag campaigns, to planning and composing posts. Because of the timely nature of social media, marketing in this field must consist of thinking on your feet and reacting in a moment's notice.

Search Engine Marketing

Maybe you've heard of this thing called Google? Everything you see on that search results page is the work of search engine marketing. Search engine marketing is an umbrella term that encompasses the two distinct fields of search engine optimization (SEO) and paid search. Search engine optimization aims to drive traffic to a website by gaining visibility in non-paid — aka "organic" — search engine results. Paid-search activities involve the paid-search ads that show up on the top of a search results page. Search engine marketing consists of managing your brand's presence on the search results page. This typically revolves around the keywords that people search for in relation to a specific brand or product.

These simple marketing tactics will help guide your business and help to build your brand. Developing a good marketing strategy will help to sustain your business and influence growth amongst new customers. Be sure to set aside a budget for marketing, as this is another component to the overall start of a new business.

The Legal Aspect

Starting a business is both exciting and challenging. After doing your research, writing a business plan, and deciding on a business structure, you'll want to consider the other legal aspects involved, so your business operates with all of the required licenses and permits. More often than not, new business owners aren't aware of these laws and unaware of what is required. Here are some important legal requirements to review and understand before launching your business:

- Registered Business Name
- Federal Taxes
- State and Local Taxes
- Business Permits and Licenses
- Business Laws and Regulations

Registered Business Name

To register your business name you'll likely register a "Doing Business As" (DBA) or "Fictitious Business Name" (FBN). This process lets your state or local government know the name you are operating your business under. This registration doesn't provide trademark protection, but it does allow you to create and use the name you want for branding purposes without having to incorporate.

If you don't register a DBA name, the name of business will default to the name of the legal owner of your business. For example, if your name is Mary Johnson and you form a consulting company, the legal name of the business will be "Mary Johnson." However, if you decide to name your company "Mary Johnson Consulting," you'll need to register this as a DBA name. Specific DBA registration rules vary from state to state. The only time you don't need to register a DBA name is if you're a sole proprietor and decide to operate under your own name. Likewise, if you do intend to create an official business structure like an LLC or corporation, your chosen business name will automatically register with the state.

If you are planning on operating nationally or providing online services, you may want to consider getting your business name trademarked. A DBA name or incorporated business name will not offer brand protection in the 49 states where your business is not registered. While trademarking is not a requirement, it will provide stronger protection for your brand. This process involves applying for a trademark with the U.S. Patent and Trademark Office. If you do want to pursue a trademark, start by conducting a comprehensive search to make sure the name you want to use is available.

Federal Taxes

Any business that operates as a corporation or partnership or has employees will need an Employer Identification Number (EIN) from the IRS. An EIN identifies your business for tax purposes — think of it like a Social Security number for your business — and you can use it to open a business bank account, file tax returns, and apply for business licenses. The easiest way to apply for an EIN is online via the IRS EIN Assistant. If you operate as a sole proprietorship, you are not required to obtain an EIN although obtaining one is a way to create additional separation between business and personal liability.

State and Local Taxes

In addition to federal taxes, businesses are also required to pay state and local taxes — self-employment, payroll, income, sales, and property tax. These taxes will vary from state-to-state and are based on your business structure. If your company has employees, you will also be responsible for paying state unemployment taxes.

Business Permits and Licenses

Just like any other business, your new business may be required to obtain proper permits and licenses. Depending on your industry and where your business is located, you may need to be licensed on the federal level as well as on the state level. Federal licenses are required for businesses involved in any sort of activity that is supervised and regulated by a federal agency. For example, if you want to create a new drug that can heal broken bones, this would require licensing by the FDA. State licensing and permits will vary depending on location.

Business Laws and Regulations

As a new business owner, you're subject to some of the laws and regulations that apply to large corporations. These include advertising, marketing, finance, intellectual property, and privacy laws. Review and understand which of these laws may apply to your business. When starting a new business, there are a lot of legal details, reports, and forms to work through to remain compliant. Be sure to conduct research in this area. Keep in mind, most businesses do not require many forms, but depending on how complex your new business is, there may be more paperwork associated with it.

Ready For Take Off

Whew! We covered quite a bit of information as it pertains to starting your business and creating your brand. Now that we have a blueprint of how to begin, it is time to get to work. This may seem like a heavy task at hand, but remember, hard work pays off in the long run. Building a business and building a brand is not an easy task and it will take a lot of dedication, time management, and patience. The best way to tackle all of this is to take it in steps. Set aside a few tasks to be completed and then accomplish them. Once you start to tackle these small tasks, you will start to see the development of your new business. Stick to your level of expertise. If there is something you do not feel comfortable doing, remember that you can always hire a professional to help. I strongly advise seeking out the help of family and friends first, as they are apart of your known resources.

Konnect FOUR hopes that this guide will help you along the way. We also offer additional services if you need assistance in conquering any of the tasks at hand. We want to see you succeed and your brand explode! Thank you for taking the time to read our guide, and we wish the best of luck in Building a Business and Building a Brand.

References

en.oxforddictionaries.com.
https://en.oxforddictionaries.com/definition/marketing

en.oxforddictionaries.com.
https://en.oxforddictionaries.com/definition/advertising

mbopartners.com.
https://www.mbopartners.com/blog/five-legal-
requirements-for-starting-a-small-business

rasmussen.edu.
https://www.rasmussen.edu/degrees/business/blog/differe
nt-types-of-marketing/